Never tell your Mother this dream

By Nicole Hollander

St. Martin's Press, New York

Book designed by
Tom Greensfelder

ISBN 0-312-56480-5

First Edition
10 9 8 7 6 5 4 3 2 1

Nicole Hollander's greeting cards are available from
The Maine Line Co., P.O. Box 418, Rockport, ME 04856. (207) 236-8536.

Think of this refrigerator as a small, locked room, housing who knows what loathsome, malignant creature.

MA, I JUST SAW
AN ENORMOUS
COCKROACH
RUN UNDER
THE DOOR, LET
ME IN, AND I'LL
SQUASH it.

Boy, you'D
SAY ANY-
THING to
GET ME
out of
--MA!
the
tub.

OH WOW, it's BIG AS A PONY.
MA, I'M Not KIDDING.
HE LIKES CORN CHIPS.
OKAY MA, I'LL take A BATH At the GAS Station.

THERAPY FOR THE DEEPLY FED-UP.

I'M TIRED OF WATCHING MY WEIGHT. LET SOMEONE ELSE WORRY ABOUT IT! DOES ORSON WELLES WORRY? DOES TIP O'NEILL DRINK TAB?

IN RESPONSE TO CRITICISM FROM CONSERVATIVES THAT T.V. NEWS IS THE CAPTIVE OF LIBERAL INTERESTS AND WORSE, WE HAVE ADDED A NIGHTLY FEATURE CALLED "IT'S ALL RIGHT" TO REINFORCE THEIR WORST FEARS.

KVETCH HERE ↑

DOES PAVAROTTI SAY: "HOLD THE BUTTER"? DOES RODNEY DANGERFIELD "GRAZE"?

GO GET A REUBEN SANDWICH AND CALL ME IN THE MORNING.

BILL BILLS JUNIOR

TODAY IN NEW YORK, THOUSANDS OF WELFARE CHEATERS GATHERED TO RECEIVE AWARDS AND CERTIFICATES OF COMMENDATION FROM LEADING DEMOCRATS.

Common Misunderstandings Between Well-meaning People

HERE'S THE ABALONE, SWEETHEART. I HAD to FLY to CALIFORNIA FOR it. AND WHAT WITH FLIGHT DELAYS AND THE TIME CHANGE it TOOK LONGER THAN I THOUGH. THEY WERE A LITTLE SURPRISED. YOU WANTED IT ON WHITE BREAD WITH MUSTARD.

"BALONEY, DEAR," I SAID, "A BALONEY SANDWICH."

A Styling Mousse is:

☐ 1. ANY ANTLERED ANIMAL WHO HAS BEEN TRAINED to CUT HAIR.

☐ 2. A PUDDING YOU EAT to MAKE YOUR HAIR CURLY.

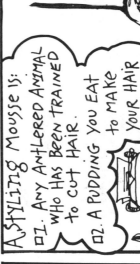

Dipped your tail in the styling mousse AGAIN, DIDN'T YOU?

HAIR THRU HIS...

AVOID EMBARRASSMENT AT the BEAUTY SHOP. KNOW YOUR TERMS.

HAIRPIN → (ARCHAIC)

AMBIGUOUS
STATEMENTS
BETWEEN
COUPLES
OFTEN
LEAD TO
QUARRELS.

I DREAMT
I WAS
MAVREEN
REAGAN.

Now there's a pill, because 2 days of the month, women change not only physically,

22

WATCH
it
grow.

No,
YOU can't
HAVE A
CHIA PET.

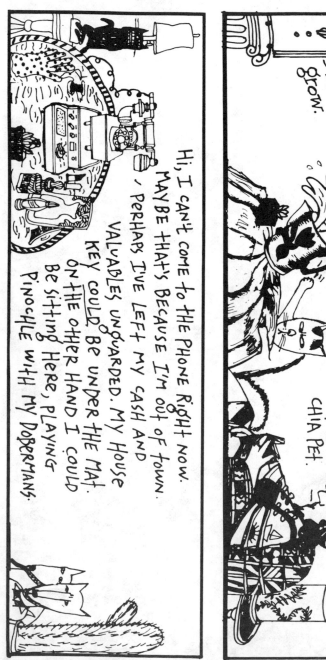

Hi, I can't come to the phone right now.
Maybe that's because I'm out of town.
, Perhaps I've left my cash and
valuables unguarded. My house
key could be under the mat.
On the other hand I could
be sitting here, playing
pinochle with my Dobermans.

Results of a survey taken among mothers sitting on the edge of a sandbox in the park

Most hated piece of movie dialogue: "Mommy, Mommy! I can't see, everything's going black."

Honey, promise me you won't play near the railroad tracks.

PEORIA

Yes, Mother I heard about the eclipse.

Yes, I know that looking into the sun during an eclipse could cause retinal damage.

Mom, since it's only a partial eclipse, do you really feel it's necessary to stay indoors for 2 days?

Something mothers only have to worry about every 20 years or so

there's nothing in this Refriger- ator that a Normal, well- Adjusted person Needs.

WHICH JOAN WOULD YOU LEAST LIKE to be TRAPPED IN A TIME WARP AND SENT BACK to the 15th CENTURY WITH? □ 1. JOAN RIVERS □ 2. JOAN CRAWFORD □ 3. JOAN OF ARC

Rita, honey, could you BRING ME A GRILLED cheese AND tomato SANDWICH, A VANILLA SHAKE AND A FEW cookies?

THE BUMPER STICKER ON MY CAR SAYS: "I BREAK FOR Unicorns AND Hobbits." YOU KNOW YOU HAVE REALLY SENSI-tive eyes.

Mine SAYS: "I ♥ MY semi-AUTOMATIC WEAPON." YOUR HAIR IS LIKE SUN-RISE ON A DUCK BLIND.

PUHLEAZE! GIVE ME A BREAK IF HE 🚫 SAW A "HOBBIT" He'd SHOOT it. YOU CRY WHEN they SHOOT "SKEET" GET AWAY FROM EACH other BEFORE I LOSE MY PATIENCE.

Love Cop: RAFING HITHER AND YON TRYING to PREVENT INCOMPATIBLE couples FROM GETTING INVOLVED.

NO, DON'T! TAKE two ASPIRIN AND CALL ME IN THE MORNING!

toDAY two Hospitals
on the west coast
instituted "PAY
As you Go Surgery."
the Surgeon and
operating Room
staff will be
coin operated.

"WE'LL HAVE DOLLAR BILL CHANGERS RIGHT IN THE O.R. — SHOULD BE NO PROBLEM," SAID A HOSPITAL ADMINISTRATOR.

Common
Misunderstandings
in
the White House.

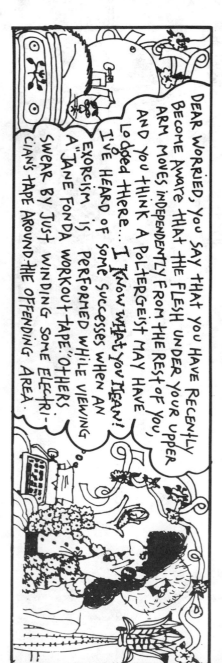

Some folks will find it difficult to get into Heaven, and they won't be pleasant about it.

The start-up of your nuclear power plant was delayed because you falsified safety tests and generally messed up, and then to top it off you want to pass the costs of the delay on to the consumer.

If you don't let me in, I'll build one right here

Mom, can a douche make you feel more confident?

Not like a good stock-portfolio.

TRANSLATION: THE KITCHEN THAT'S NEVER USED REMAINS FOREVER NEW.
DID YOU REDO YOUR KITCHEN; IT LOOKS TERRIFIC?
KITCHEN? IS THAT WHAT THIS ROOM IS CALLED?

RESEARCHERS IN AROMATHERAPY SAY THAT THE 'SMELL OF PINE OR OF APPLE, CAN RELIEVE ANXIETY.

THAT'S NOTHING....

the SMELL OF PIZZA CAN RAISE the DEAD.

MA, THAT'S SACRILEGIOUS.

Lives of Susan

COMEDY MINI-SERIES ABOUT A WOMAN WITH A 3-WAY SPLIT PERSONALITY: WAITRESS, HOUSEWIFE AND GOURMET.

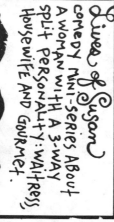

SUSAN'S HUSBAND IS TEASING HER ABOUT HOW SHE PROBABLY WON'T BE ABLE to CLAIM A PERSONAL DEDUCTION FOR EACH OF HER MULTIPLE PERSONALITIES, WHEN SUSAN'S FISCAL ANXIETY BRINGS FORTH HER GOURMET PERSONA AND SHE EATS THE KITCHEN WALLPAPER.

I DREAMT THE DOLLAR COLLAPSED — AND THE MEDIUM OF EXCHANGE WAS OLD COMIC BOOKS.

MOST OF THE WORRY ABOUT COMPUTERS CENTERS ON HOW THEY CAN BE USED FOR ILLEGAL PUR-POSES, BUT A POTENTIALLY MORE DISTURBING PROBLEM HAS ARISEN.

DOC, I HAVE CARNAL FEELINGS ABOUT MY COMPUTER.
CRY
WASN'T IT YOUR FAMILY WHO ADOPTED A CUISINART?

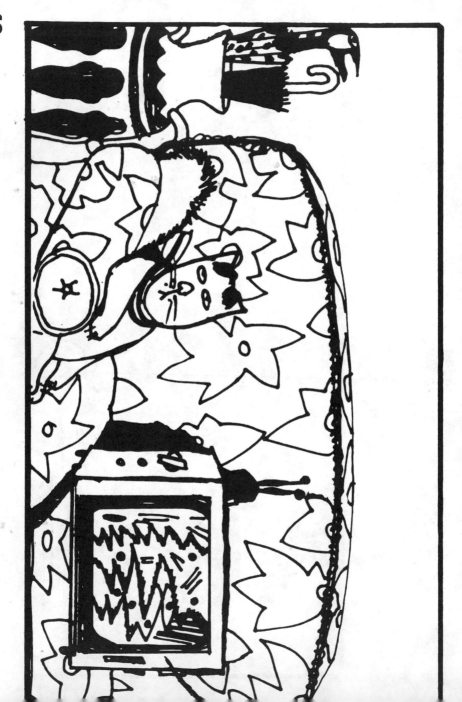

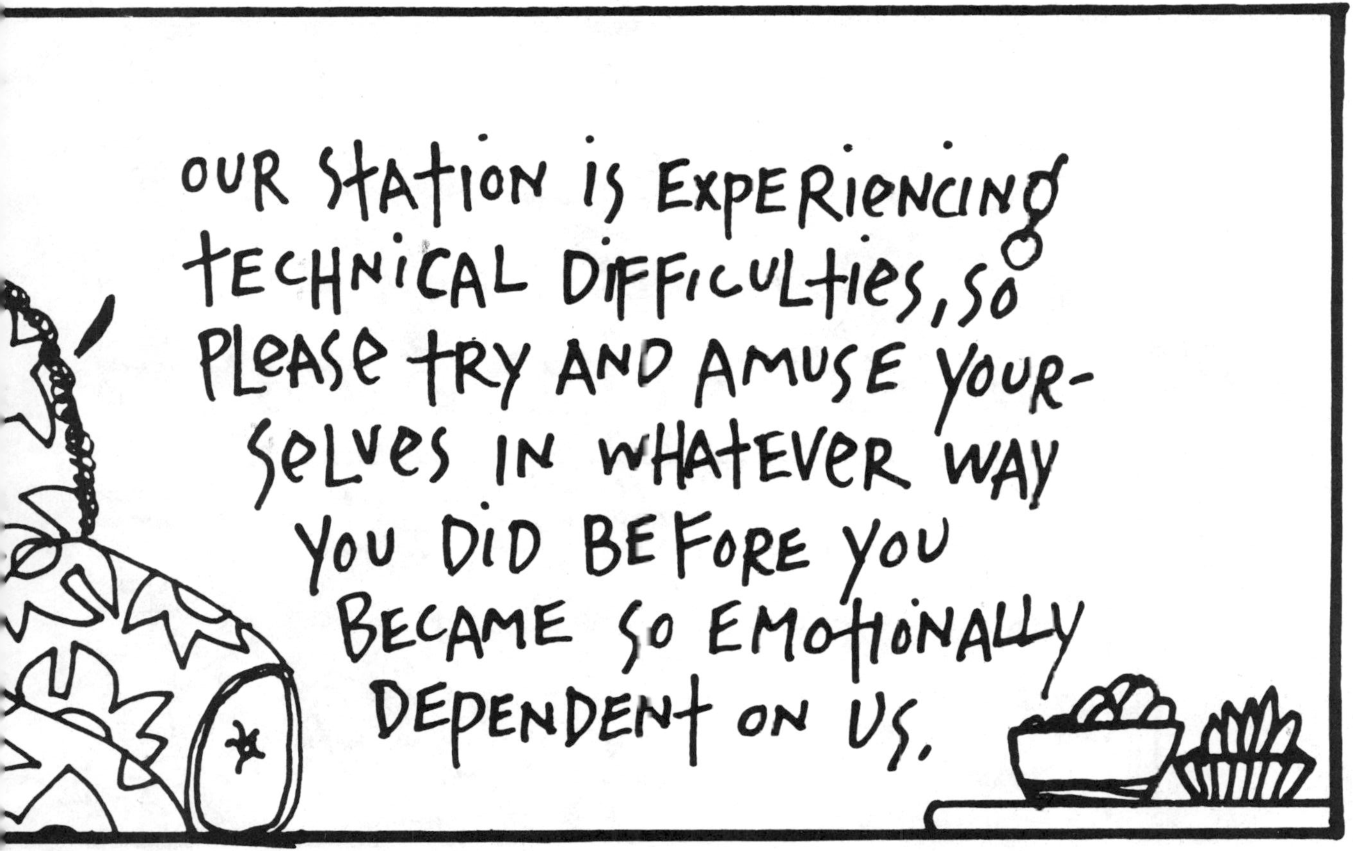

OUR STATION IS EXPERIENCING
TECHNICAL DIFFICULTIES, SO
PLEASE TRY AND AMUSE YOUR-
SELVES IN WHATEVER WAY
YOU DID BEFORE YOU
BECAME SO EMOTIONALLY
DEPENDENT ON US.

THE CRYSTAL BALL ISN'T WARMED UP YET. CHECK OUT THE FORTUNE COOKIES.

SURVEY QUESTION ASKED OF PEOPLE AT AN ALL-NIGHT PHARMACY.

"YOUR DEAREST WISH WILL COME TRUE." I THINK THERE'S ANOTHER FORTUNE STUCK INSIDE.

"AND YOU'LL BE SORRY." I HATE IT WHEN THEY GET PHILOSOPHICAL.

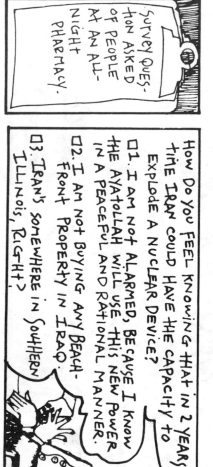

How Do You FEEL KNOWING THAT IN 2 YEARS TIME IRAN COULD HAVE THE CAPACITY TO EXPLODE A NUCLEAR DEVICE?

□1. I AM NOT ALARMED, BECAUSE I KNOW THE AYATOLLAH WILL USE THIS NEW POWER IN A PEACEFUL AND RATIONAL MANNER.

□2. I AM NOT BUYING ANY BEACH-FRONT PROPERTY IN IRAQ.

□3. IRAN'S SOMEWHERE IN SOUTHERN ILLINOIS, RIGHT?

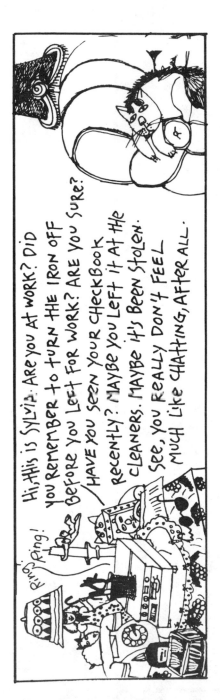

RING, Ring!

Hi, this is Sylvia. Are you at work? Did you remember to turn the iron off before you left for work? Are you sure? Have you seen your checkbook recently? Maybe you left it at the cleaners. Maybe it's been stolen. See, you really don't feel much like chatting, after all...

It's the perfect time to buy real estate because no one even knows what "real estate" is. Right now you could buy property in Manhattan for a song.

Last night I had a dream about the Russian Tea Room.

The snake talks Adam and Eve into buying property.

Hi Mom. Yes I was out. I picked up my new reading glasses.

Mom, don't cry. No Mom, I won't tell anyone I wear reading glasses. I didn't tell anyone I was 30, did I Mom?

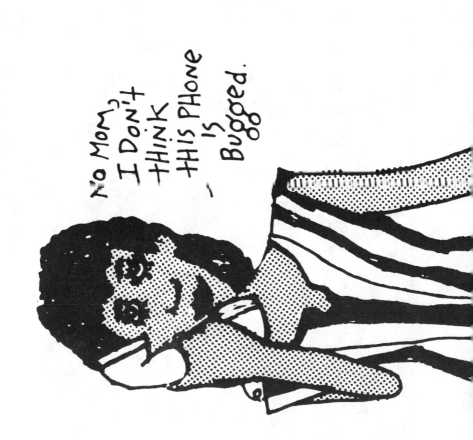

You do it just to irritate me, don't you?

SYLVIA'S Encyclopedia of Little Known Diseases

TRANCEO'FOOD (Latin name)

UNCONSCIOUS EATING (Laymen's term)

A SUFFERER SPEAKS: "Often the first thing I notice is that my jaws are moving. Then I look down at my hand and there's a piece of coffee cake in it."

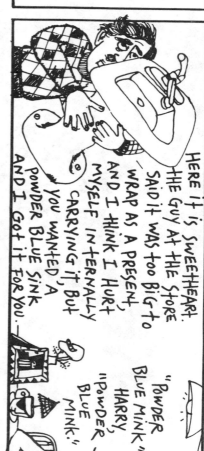

HERE it is SWEETHEART. The guy at the store said it was too big to wrap as a present, and I think I hurt myself internally carrying it, but you wanted a powder blue sink and I got it for you.

"POWDER BLUE MINK" Harry. "POWDER BLUE MINK."

ANOTHER SUFFERER SPEAKS "I was driving 85 miles per hour on the freeway when I noticed I was eating. I was completely baffled. Then I saw that my glove compartment was stuffed with chili dogs.

Lives of Susan

COMEDY MINI-SERIES ABOUT
A WOMAN WHO HAS A 3-WAY
SPLIT PERSONALITY: SURGEON,
WAITRESS, AND CHIHUAHUA

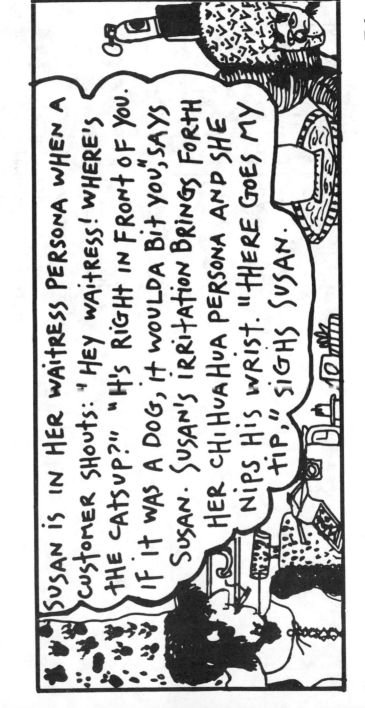

SUSAN IS IN HER WAITRESS PERSONA WHEN A CUSTOMER SHOUTS: "HEY WAITRESS! WHERE'S THE CATSUP?" "IT'S RIGHT IN FRONT OF YOU. IF IT WAS A DOG, IT WOULDA BIT YOU," SAYS SUSAN. SUSAN'S IRRITATION BRINGS FORTH HER CHIHUAHUA PERSONA AND SHE NIPS HIS WRIST. "THERE GOES MY TIP," SIGHS SUSAN.

Look ALL I'M SAYING is if we AS A NATION KEEP DIETING, WE REDUCE PERSONAL SPENDING ON FOOD AND SLOW DOWN THE Economic Recovery.

So you're SAYING "CHUBBY" is PATRIOTIC?

UFO LANDS ON SMERF

You COULD PUT IT THAT WAY.

HARRY, A ROUND OF CHEESECAKE FOR ME AND MY PAL.

Liz DATE Jackie

"Come see what I Got For You," He called from the other Room. "It Better Be good, I said, it Better Be some thing like Placido DOMINGO AND BARYSHNIKOV Here to Do A SONG AND DANCE."

IF FROGS HAVE Teeth, Do THEY get CAVITIES?

"OH, you GUESSED," He SIGHED.

A Lien Love... Can A woman from a small Town in the Mid- west Find Joy on Another PLANET?

OH, LOVER.

ANGEL.

Love Cops: FLYING ALL OVER THE PLANET TO NIP INCOMPATIBLE MALE/FEMALE RELATIONSHIPS IN THE BUD.
WAIT! FLIRTING WITH THE WRONG PERSON CAN BE INJURIOUS TO YOUR HEALTH.

A young man and woman in Boston teeter on the brink of disaster.

AND I HAVE A CAT CALLED "MARCEL PROUST."

I'VE GOT TWO DOBERMANS — NAMED "SUDDEN DEATH". OH, YOUR EYES ARE Sooo BLUE.

Whew! Love Cop's Here! GIRL, GO HOME. YOUR KITTY LITTER NEEDS ATTENTION. AND YO, FELLAH, YOUR DOGS ATE ANOTHER POST MAN. SKEDATTLE!

"SHE READ EVERY PIECE OF DIRECT MAIL SOLICITATION SHE RECEIVED."

"SHE NEVER WENT INTO THE '8 ITEMS — OR LESS' LINE IN THE SUPER-MARKET WITH MORE THAN 8 ITEMS."

I DREAMT THAT I WAS OFFERED $100,000 IF I COULD ANSWER ONE QUESTION. THE QUESTION WAS "WHO WOULD YOU TAKE WITH YOU TO THE MOON?" WHILE I WAS DEBATING THE PROS AND CONS OF MEL GIBSON, GRACE JONES, AND CARL SAGAN, I NOTICED THAT I HADN'T PROPERLY ZIPPED UP MY JEANS. SUDDENLY A VOICE SAID: "TIME'S UP, YOU LOSE."

59

LITTLE KNOWN POLLUTANTS

MA, WHAT'S ALL THAT STUFF IN THE AIR?

...THOSE ARE WRINKLES ARTHUR... QUICK, CLOSE THE WINDOW!

MY BACK HURTS, I HATE MY JOB, NO ONE APPRECIATES ME, MY CAR'S BEEN NOTHING BUT TROUBLE SINCE I GOT IT, THIS PUPPY NEVER LEAVES ME ALONE.

SWEET HEART, I DIDN'T SAY: "WHINE". I SAID I WANTED A GLASS OF WINE.

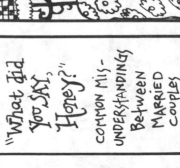

"What did you say, Honey?"

COMMON MIS-UNDERSTANDINGS BETWEEN MARRIED COUPLES

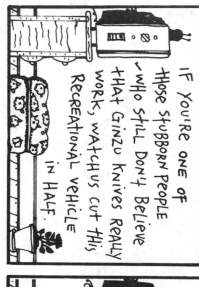

IF YOU'RE ONE OF those stubborn people ~ who still don't believe that Ginzu knives really work, watch us cut this recreational vehicle in HALF.

See! the Ginzu ~ knife does it easily and still cuts this radish into razor-thin slices.

Still not convinced? Okay, we're on our ~ way to Washington D.C. to cut the Lincoln Memorial into bite-size pieces.

Syl's Writing School ~ today: Writing Headlines For the National Enquirer.

See how many headlines you can make using combinations of words or phrases below.
1. Boy
2. Mother
3. Weds
4. Alligator
5. Raised by wild apes.

SYLVIA'S Etiquette tips FOR the FASTIDIOUS WOMAN.

A REAL LADY NEVER SAYS: "OH MY GOSH, I FORGOT to TURN ON MY ANSWERING MACHINE, I'LL BE BACK IN ABOUT 20 MINUTES", DURING A PASSIONATE EMBRACE.

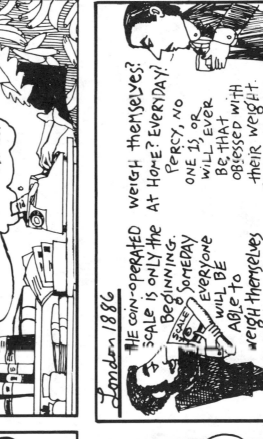

London 1886

THE COIN-OPERATED SCALE IS ONLY THE BEGINNING. SOMEDAY EVERYONE WILL BE ABLE TO WEIGH THEMSELVES AT HOME, EVERYDAY.

WEIGH THEMSELVES AT HOME? EVERYDAY? PERCY, NO ONE IS, OR WILL EVER BE THAT OBSESSED WITH THEIR WEIGHT. IT ISN'T DECENT.

PERCIVAL EVERETT TALKS OVER HIS INVENTION OF THE COIN-OPERATED WEIGHT MACHINE WITH A PAL.

Getting into
Heaven will
Be Difficult
for Some
Authors.

Let's see. You're
the author of
that wonder-
ful story
about the
two boys
who save
a family
of rabbits,
right?

Actually I wrote
that CIA manual
that contains
suggestions for
neutralizing
the Nicaraguans
through the
selective use
of violence.

ARE YOUR CHILDREN ASKING QUESTIONS that MAKE YOU SQUIRM? SEND FOR MY FREE "NOT A CABBAGE-PATCH DOLL" BROCHURE.

THE DOLLS ARE PROGRAMMED to GIVE YOUR CHILD STRAIGHTFORWARD ANSWERS to QUESTIONS You DON'T WANT to DISCUSS.

Hi. MY NAME is POLLY, AND I'M GOING to TELL YOU ABOUT THE DEFICIT... BUT FIRST I'M GOING to SING "OLD MACDONALD'S FARM."

Just PULL THE CORD BEHIND THE DOLL'S EAR.

The way
it probably
really
HAPPened.

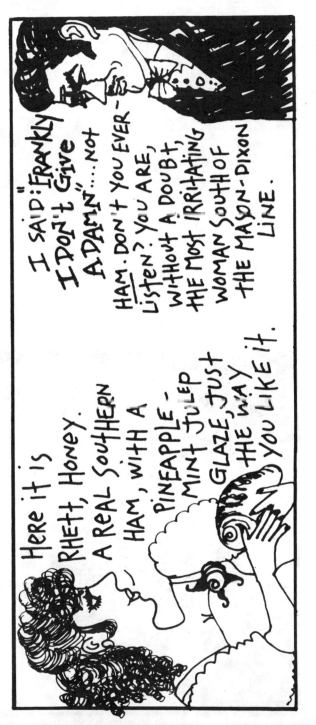

It's like you go to a Van Halen concert and you're the oldest person there, and there's a mix-up in the tickets, and you have to stand for the whole thing and it's hot and the kid next to you loses his lunch on your shoe.

OH NO!

I know. You thought it was going to be witty and Noel Cowardish.

Excuse me, I have to go home and give my possessions to charity.

74

Mini Quiz
What food puts on weight, if you even look at it?

"If you can read this, you're too close."

Pick the correct meaning of the word "Strident"
☐1. A sugarless gum.
☐2. A woman who speaks out for equality.
☐3. A nuclear-powered submarine.

WHICH of these RUMORS is totally Unfounded?
☐1 Video games make you sterile.
☐2. In 1935 Freud made a secret trip to the U.S. to treat the Rockettes who were suddenly unable to kick in unison.
☐3. Masters and Johnson are sister and brother.

DEAR WORRIED IN WICHITA, It HAS ALWAYS BEEN MY PERSONAL BELIEF THAT THERE WILL BE A SMOKING SECTION IN HEAVEN, BUT IT'LL BE SMALL.

It's Horrible! I can't eat it.

ingenious.

Ruby, how can you call this a "Diet Plate"? — It's a Pork chop with mashed potatoes and gravy.

Just taste it.

At Breakfast Susan's husband is quietly picking cat hairs out of his cereal when Susan's rage at this implied criticism of her housekeeping standards, brings out her taxidermist persona, and she attempts to stuff and mount her husband to the south wall of the breakfast nook.

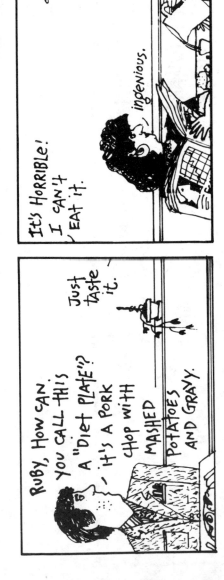

Lives of Susan comedy mini-series about a woman who has a split personality: house-wife, waitress, taxidermist.

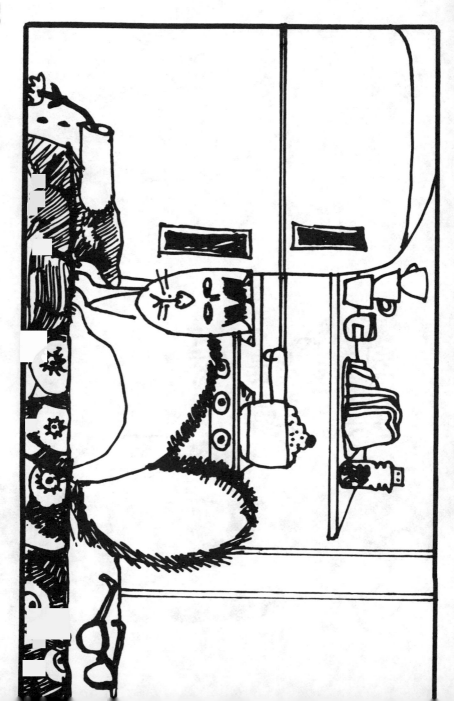

HARRY, YOU REMEMBER THOSE ALMOND COOKIES I MAKE — THE ONES THAT TASTE SO GOOD WHEN YOU DIP THEM IN COFFEE?

OH YEAH, THE "KILLER" COOKIES! WHAT ABOUT 'EM? LAST NIGHT...

WE DON'T SERVE SMURFS.

CATS IN SPACE!

I ATE FIVE HUNDRED.

MEDIEVAL TALES OF LOVE AND PASSION.

FAIR MAIDEN, SHOW ME THE DRAGON THAT I — MIGHT SLAY HIM TO PROVE MY LOVE FOR THEE... —YONDER.

OKAY. SHOW ME A SMALLER ONE.

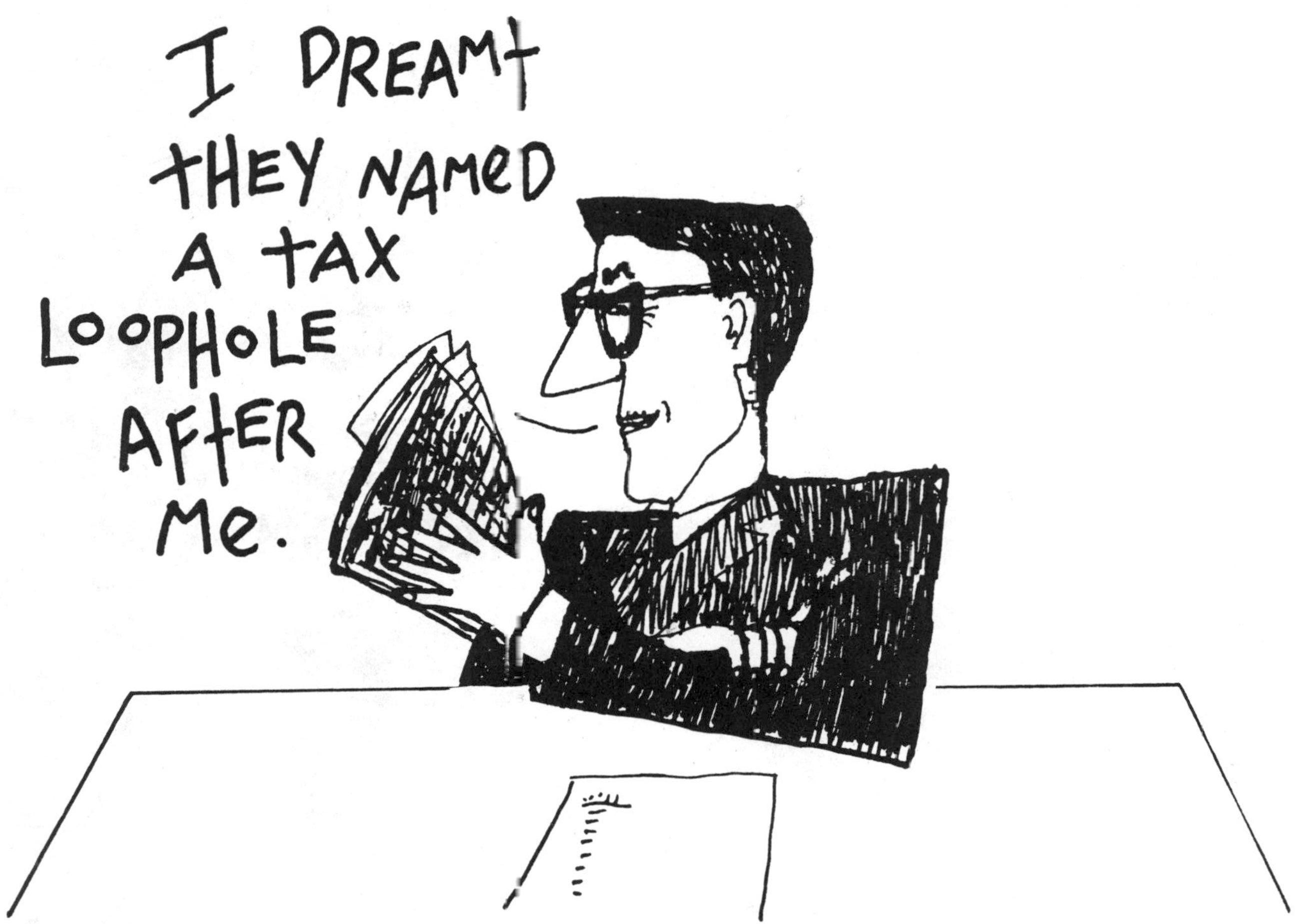
I DREAMT
THEY NAMED
A TAX
LOOPHOLE
AFTER
ME.

"WELL I HAVE A SURPRISE FOR YOU," HE SMILED AND OPENED A SLIDING PANEL TO REVEAL A FULLY-EQUIPPED LAB WITH TWO ASSISTANTS. "I THOUGHT YOU MIGHT LIKE TO DO A LITTLE GENETIC ENGINEERING." "WOW!" I SAID, AND FELL INTO HIS ARMS, ARMS, ARMS.

"YOU'RE BORED MY SWEET," HE MURMURED AS HE WATCHED ME UNRAVEL THE ANGORA SWEATER I WAS WEARING. "IT'S TRUE, SINCE I FINISHED MY EPIC POEM ON THE I.R.S., I HAVE BEEN AT LOOSE ENDS," I SIGHED.

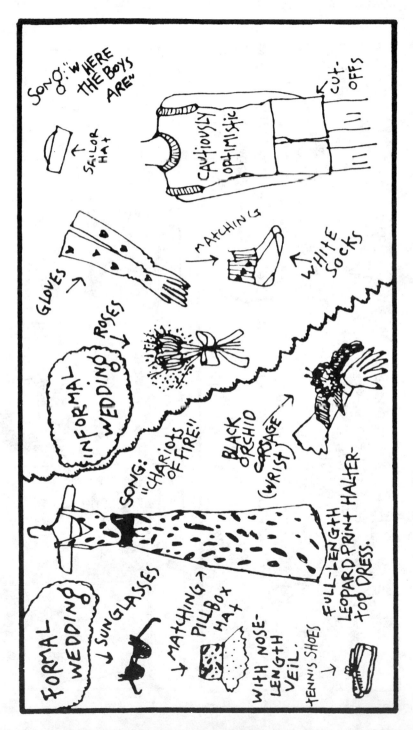

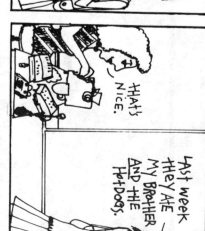

Sylvia's Information Center.

HOW COME PEOPLE CONTINUE TO GET SUNTANS EVEN THOUGH THEY KNOW THE SUN'S RAYS ARE HARMFUL?

Most Frequently Asked Question

WHAT IS THE MOST BEAUTIFUL SOUND IN THE WORLD?

☐ 1. A BABY'S LAUGH.
☐ 2. A CHECK BEING REMOVED FROM AN ENVELOPE.

ANSWER: HOT FUDGE BEING POURED OVER ICE-CREAM.

SOME PEOPLE CONFUSE LOOKING HEALTHY WITH BEING HEALTHY. SORTA LIKE A METAPHOR FOR OUR ECONOMIC RECOVERY.

MY BOYFRIEND AND I FIGHT EVERY TIME WE COOK A MEAL TOGETHER.

WALLPAPER OVER YOUR PROBLEMS

EAT OUT.

WORDS TO LIVE BY.

BUT THAT JUST AVOIDS THE REAL PROBLEM.

FAMOUS Movie MisunDer-Standings

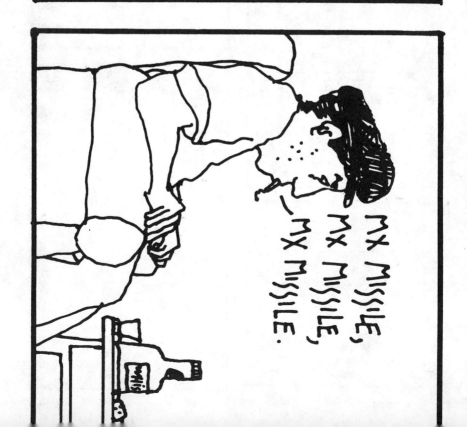

MX MISSILE,
MX MISSILE,
— MX MISSILE.

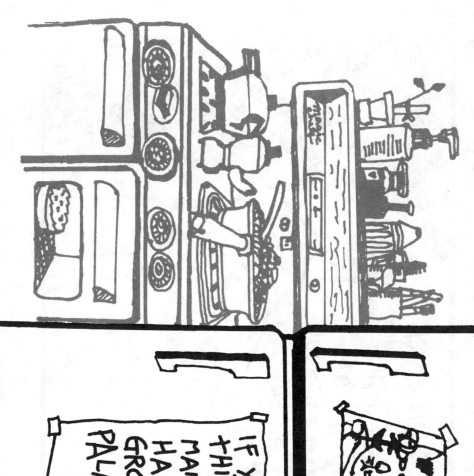

IF YOU OPEN THIS DOOR TOO MANY TIMES, HAIR WILL GROW ON THE PALMS OF YOUR HANDS.

Select the correct use of the word "Quark" in the sentences below.

☐1. "Quark, what light from yonder window breaks?"

☐2. "I heard a faint 'Quark, Quark, Quark' from the direction of the lily pond."

☐3. "Wearing shoes in the shower is more than a mental quark, it's downright weird."

Sylvia's Bonus "Quark" word:

Quarks are very, very small and can only be seen by people who play chess and never get a tan.

I feel badly about this, so I'm throwing in the ability to find parking on a Saturday, anywhere in the U.S. and Canada.

It's my soul.

The Devil hesitates to take advantage of a man with a bad cold.

...this doesn't seem like a good deal for you.

You're willing to hand over your immortal soul in exchange for no more colds.....?

I don't want any more colds.

Heavy Duty

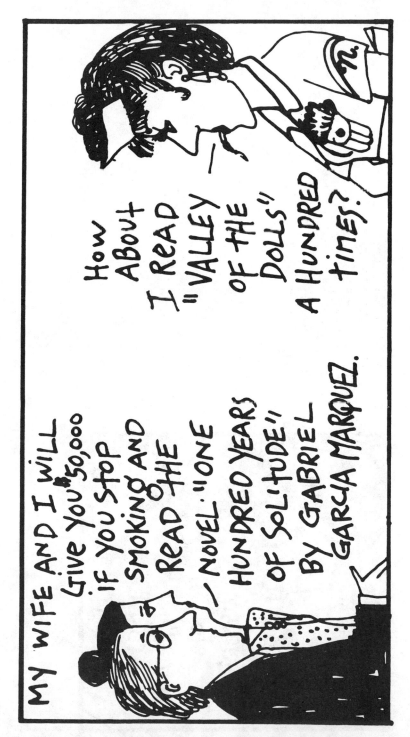

LITTLE KNOWN NICKNAMES OF Historical Figures.

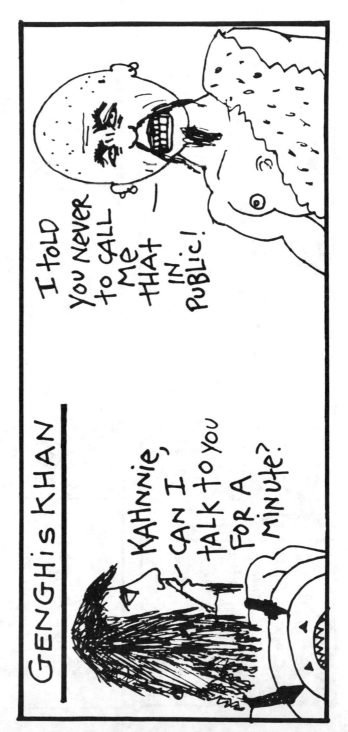

WAS THE SAME ANNE BURFORD WHO RESIGNED, UNDER A CLOUD, FROM THE EPA. "WE'RE NOT THAT DUMB," SAID A WHITE HOUSE SPOKESMAN.

THE WHITE HOUSE DENIED TODAY THAT THE ANNE BURFORD NAMED LAST MONTH TO HEAD A NATIONAL ADVISORY COMMITTEE ON THE ENVIRONMENT

Nervous HABiT #1

Vicki BEGiNS TO UNRAVEL HER SWEATER AS HER HUSBAND TELLS HiS UFO STORY FOR THE 700TH TiME.

FiRST THERE WAS THiS BLiNDING LIGHT AND THEN THE ELECTRICAL SYSTEM IN THE CAR CONKED OUT.

Close RELATIONSHIPS SOMETIMES CAUSE STRESS, RESULTING IN UNCONSCIOUS ACTIONS OR "TICKS".

Question
Asked At All-
Night Tanning
Parlor.

Common Misunderstandings in Ancient Rome

ARE MY TOGAS AS WHITE AS THEY COULD BE? ARE THE GODS HAPPY WITH ME? IS IT A GOOD TIME TO BUY A VILLA IN POMPEII? AM I BRUSHING LONG ENOUGH?

I DREAMT I DIED
AND WENT TO
HEAVEN AND THEY
HANDED ME SOME
OLD MS. MAGAZINES,
A PAPER SHEET,
AND MADE ME
SIT IN A LITTLE
ROOM WITH
A BUNCH
OF OTHER
DOCTORS.

I'M SICK OF IT! ANOTHER SEMINAR TO TEACH BUSINESS WOMEN ~ SPORTS AND WAR TERMS SO THEY CAN SOUND LIKE MEN... "ARMED TO THE TEETH"

OPEN-TOED SHOES AND DANGLE EARRINGS ARE A NO NOS IN THE BUSINESS WORLD

"BLOODIED, BUT UNBOWED!" FEH! WHEN ARE THEY GOING TO TEACH MEN TO ~ SAY STUFF LIKE: "THIS DEAL'S AS WOBBLY AS A GIRAFFE IN FOUR INCH HEELS!"?

BATTEN THE HATCHES! GUYS, SHE'S ON THE WARPATH.

COULD WHAT YOUR CHILD ~ EATS TODAY CAUSE A HEART ATTACK WHEN HE'S 45?

AND COULD HE SUE YOU?

COFFEE INCOMPATIBILITY IS A MINE FIELD!

MORE ARGUMENTS ARE SETTLED OVER COFFEE — THAN IN BED. Listen to me when I TALK to you!

I CAN'T WAIT to take you to Nick's. THEY MAKE THE BEST CAFÉ LATTÉ IN TOWN.

I NEVER touch ANYTHING WITH CAFFEINE IN IT.

Love Cop: IN HER never ending Battle to keep incompatible couples from Romantic involvement, Love cop sometimes gets irritable.

I DO NOT!

WARNING SIGNS: 1. You can only close the zipper on your jeans by using an enormous safety pin. 2. You manage to zip up your jeans, But moments later you lose all feeling in your lower body. You beg a friend to cut off your pants.

GET OFF!

How to TELL IF YOU ARE OVERWEIGHT.

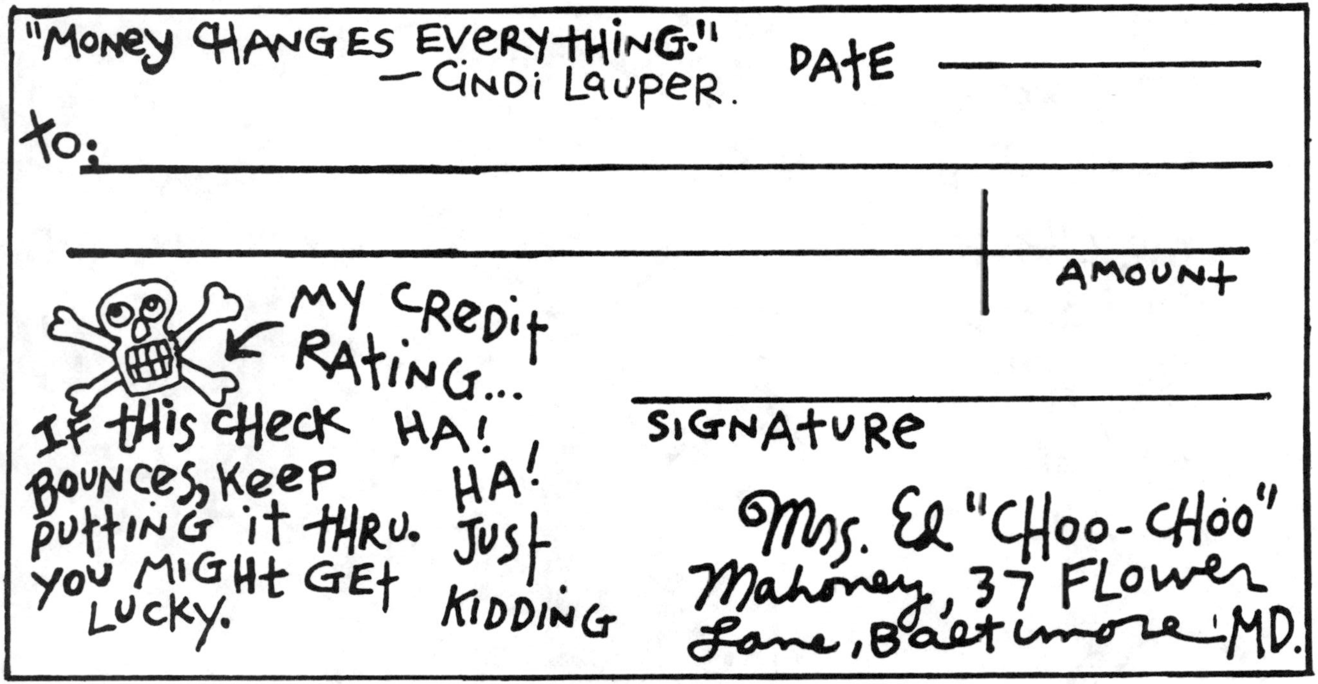

"Money Changes Everything."
—Cindi Lauper.

To:

Date

Amount

Signature

Mrs. El "Choo-Choo" Mahoney, 37 Flower Lane, Baltimore, MD.

← My credit rating...
Ha! Ha!
If this check bounces, keep putting it thru. Just you might get lucky. Kidding

Mrs. Rosemary Davis with the check designed for her

BY Sylvia.

I'M A VERY ROMANTIC WOMAN, AND I WANTED MY CHECKS TO REFLECT THAT.

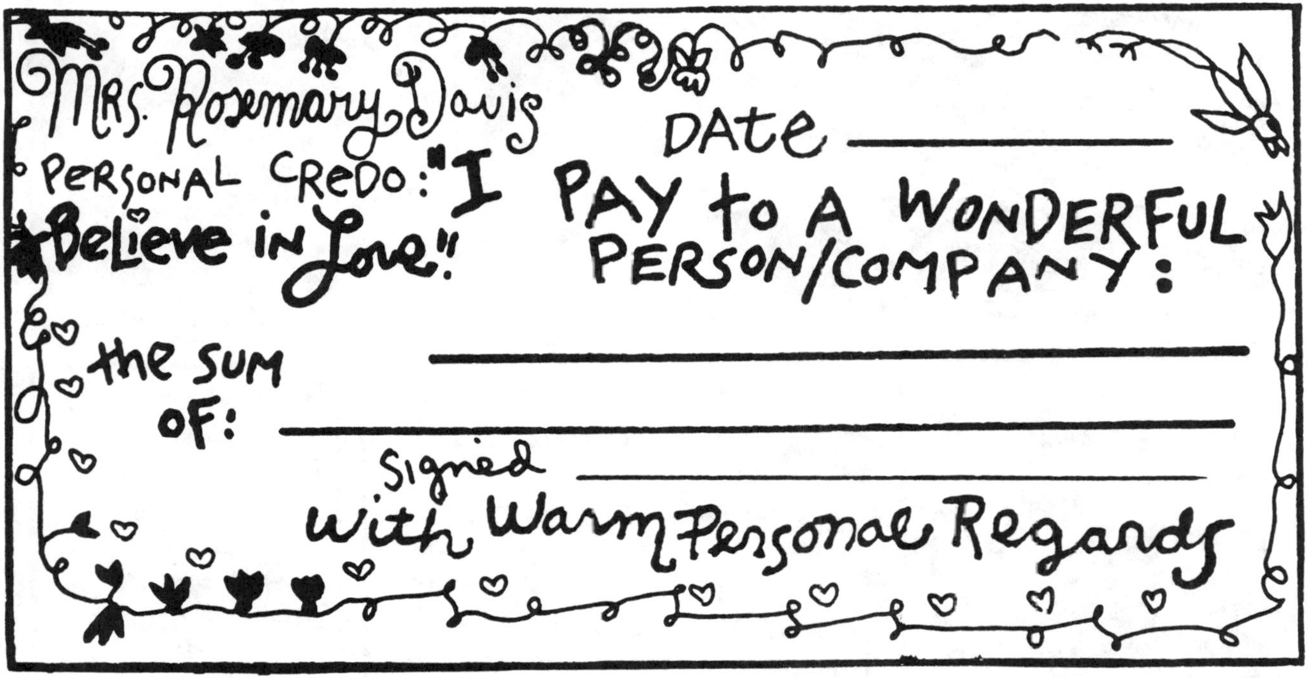

Mrs. Rosemary Davis

Personal Credo: "I Believe in Love!!"

DATE _____

PAY to A WONDERFUL PERSON/COMPANY:

the SUM OF:

Signed _____

with Warm, Personal Regards

HARRY, iF I NEVER READ ANoTHER LiNE ABouT "YuPPiES" AGAiN, IT'LL Be too SooN.

IS tHAT WHAT CollEGE KiDS ARE SWALLoWing Now?

HARRY, DID I TELL You FRANCO DIED?

☐1. tHAT WoMAN is Sick.

☐2. tHAT WoMAN is A SLoW READER.

☐3. I WouLDn't USE tHAT PAPER to LiNE A BiRDCAGE.

ARE You ADDicted to tHE NATioNAL ENQuiRER oR WHAt?

I FiGuRE I'LL Just READ it WHiLE I'M STANDiNG iN LiNE, But tHEN I SEE A HEADLiNE LikE: "I Found MY LoNG-LosT SiSTER-AND SHE StoLE MY HuSBAND," AND I BuY tHE MAGAZiNE AND READ it iN tHE CAR.

MA CAN WE Go HoME?

I'M LEAViNG—

PICK THE CORRECT USE OF THE WORD BELOW.

1. "WHADDAYAH MEAN 'ARCANE'?" HE SHOUTED, GIVING ME A VIOLENT SHOVE, "THAT'S MY CANE!"

2. "HAVE SOME OF ARCANE," HE MURMURED, "IT'S ALMOST AS SWEET AS YOU." HE FLASHED HIS DAZZLING LATIN SMILE, AND I FELT MY POLITICAL LOYALTIES SHIFT DANGEROUSLY.

BONUS WORD OF THE WEEK: ARCANE.

WE NEEDED SPACE FOR THE MALL...

IT'S SMALLER THAN I REMEMBER.

WHAT IF ADAM AND EVE WENT BACK TO EDEN?

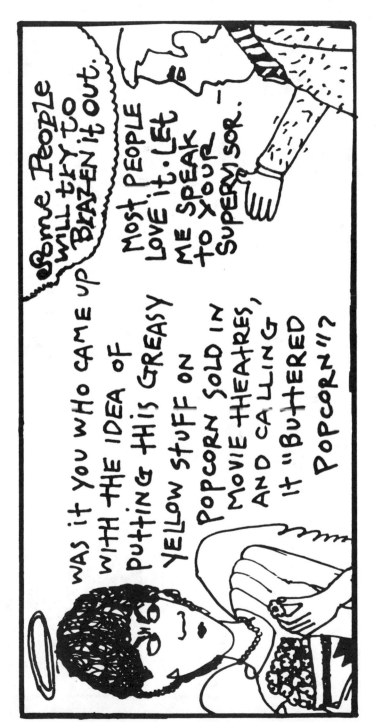

THE DEFICIT IS NOT A NEW PROBLEM. THE FIRST MENTION OF IT APPEARS IN A 16TH CENTURY PLAY.

"IS THIS A DEFICIT I SEE BEFORE ME, THE HANDLE TOWARD MY HAND?"

DUE TO POOR TRANSLATION, THE WORD "DEFICIT" HAS COME DOWN TO US AS "DAGGER", RIDICULOUS, CONSIDERING THE CONTEXT.

YOUR SEAT BELT IS FASTENED, AND YOUR KNUCKLES ARE WHITE IN ANTICIPATION OF TAKEOFF WHEN THE PILOT ANNOUNCES THE FLIGHT IS BEING DELAYED BECAUSE OF A "MAINTENANCE" PROBLEM...

WHAT DO YOU IMAGINE THEY ARE DOING TO THE PLANE?

☐1. APPLYING SUPER GLUE TO ONE OF THE WINGS.

☐2. "I DON'T CARE WHAT THEY'RE DOING, I'M LEAVING."

What if Heaven was only open to people who had the same taste in Movies as the officer of the day?

Do you AGREE --tHAt "terms of ENDEARMENT" AND "E.t." were two of tHE Best Movies ever MADE?

"ERASER-HEAD" AND "Gone with tHE WIND" ARE MY FAVORITEs.

PReVeNTiNG
NUCLEAR
WAR iS
THE <u>ONLY</u>
iSSUE.

WHAt
ABoUt
ReAGAN?
EL SALVADOR?
PoVeRTy?

Hi Mom.

Yes, I was just going to eat some yogurt. Uh huh, it's past the expiration date on the carton.

Die instantly? No, I didn't know that.

Love Quiz

THE 3 WARNING SIGNS OF TOTAL RAPTURE.

☐1. I've noticed that I've become less intelligent.

☐2. My friends have noticed.

☐3. Blue Cross/Blue Shield has cancelled my policy.

COMPLETE THE FOLLOWING SENTENCE AND THEN WRITE 300 MORE PAGES.

"I RELIVE THAT EVENING AT FAIRHAVEN CASTLE EVERY NIGHT IN MY DREAMS, FOR IT WAS THERE THAT I LOST MY...
□ INNOCENCE."
□ CONTACT LENSES IN LORD MANDINGO'S CONSOMMÉ"
□ POISE, AND, ALMOST, MY LIFE."

THINK OF THIS REFRIGERATOR AS A SMALL LOCKED ROOM HIDING WHO KNOWS WHAT KIND OF GROTESQUE, MALIGNANT CREATURE.

the SYLVIA School of Mystery Writing

"DOWN-UNDER WEAR." PUNK.

DO YOU GIVE UP? YES.

OKAY, "WHAT DO YOU CALL THE GARMENT THAT AUSTRALIAN GEESE WEAR CLOSEST TO THEIR FEATHERS?" YOU'RE MAKING THIS UP.

VERY TRIVIAL PURSUITS

SO I'M STANDING IN THE MOONLIGHT WAITING FOR HIM TO SAY SOMETHING LIKE: "YOU ARE AS LUMINOUS AND MYSTERIOUS AS THE MOON TO ME!"
WE WILL LISTEN TO THE SAME COMPLAINTS OVER AND OVER AGAIN
SO WHAT DID HE SAY?
REPETITIOUS COMPLAINT THERAPY

Other Sylvia books :

For more information about the Sylvia doll contact:

MARTHA-MY-DEAR
4169 Emerald St.
Oakland, CA 94609
(415) 658-3386

ISBN	QUANTITY	TITLE	PRICE
371934	_____	Hi, This is Sylvia	$4.95
401655	_____	I'm in Training to be Tall and Blonde	$4.95
501706	_____	Ma, can I be a Feminist and St ll Like Men?	$4.95
530137	_____	Mercy, it's the Revolution and I'm in my Bathrobe	$4.95
558619	_____	My Weight is Always Perfect for my Height	$4.95
781857	_____	Sylvia on Sundays	$4.95
795106	_____	That Woman Must be on Drugs	$4.95
583186	_____	Okay, Thinner Thighs for Everyone	$4.95

Send check for price of book plus $1.50 for postage and handling
(please add 25¢ for each additional book) to:

St. Martin's Press, Cash Sales Dept.
175 Fifth Ave., New York, NY 10010